ANDERSON

SWIMMING

How to Play the All-Star Way

By **Barry Wilner**

Introduction by **Sam Freas**

Illustrated by **Art Seiden**

Photographs by **Dan Helms and others**

★ An **Arvid Knudsen** book ★

RSVP

**RAINTREE
STECK-VAUGHN**
P U B L I S H E R S
The Steck-Vaughn Company

Austin, Texas

Acknowledgments

It takes many people to put together a book such as this. I would especially like to thank Paul Montella, Matt Farrell, and Art Cassidy. Mostly, I'd like to express my appreciation to my wife Helene, daughters Nicole, Jamie, and Tricia, and son Evan, for their help and understanding.

Photograph from the collection of Barry Wilner, p.4.
Photograph, p. 5, by J. E. Clark Photographers.
Photographs from the collection of the
International Swimming Hall of Fame, pp. 6 and 44,
with thanks to Preston Levi, Director of the Henning Library,
for his attentive assistance.
Photographs from the collection of
United States Swimming, pp. 9, 17, 20, 22, 25, 26, 29, 36, 38, 40, and 45.
Photographs by Dan Helms pp. 17 (bottom), 22,
25, 26 (top), 38, and 40 (bottom).
Photographs by Charlie Snyder, pp. 9, 20, and 40 (top).
Photographs by Walter Iooss, p. 26 (bottom).
Photographs from the collection of Mary Pat Boron, cover and p. 30.

Published by Raintree Steck-Vaughn Publishers, an imprint of
Steck-Vaughn Company.

Library of Congress Cataloging-in-Publication Data
Wilner, Barry.
Swimming / by Barry Wilner;
introduction by Sam Freas;
illustrated by Art Seiden; photographs by Dan Helms.
p. cm. — (How to play the all-star way)
"An Arvid Knudson Book."
Includes bibliographical references and index.
Summary: An introduction to competitive swimming,
covering safety concerns, various strokes, racing techniques, and more.
ISBN 0-8114-6596-9
1. Swimming—Juvenile literature. [1. Swimming]
I. Seiden, Art, ill. II. Title. III. Series.
GV837.W54 1996
797.2'1—dc20   95-46142 CIP AC

Printed and bound in the United States

1 2 3 4 5 6 7 8 9 0   99 98 97 96

CONTENTS

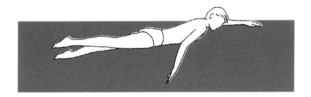

INTRODUCTION

Sam Freas

Swimming is the most popular recreational activity in the country. However, becoming a race swimmer involves much more than jumping into a pool and trying to get to the other end as fast as you can.

Throughout history, swimming has been an important part of everyone's lives. Even early Greek, Hebrew, and Muslim teachings speak of the importance of knowing how to swim. Perhaps it was best stated by the famous philosopher Plato when he said, "A man is not learned until he can read, write, and swim."

Learning to swim improves a person's self-assurance. It provides a lifetime leisure activity and the general well-being of an individual. As with any activity, a swimmer starts slowly, then goes on to learn other techniques and strokes.

The swimmer learns to dive into the pool to begin a race, and how to turn at the end of a lap. A swimmer learns how to breathe the right way, and he or she learns about safety.

Barry Wilner's book, *Swimming: How to Play the All-Star Way*, explains all about being a competitive swimmer. Someday, maybe you will be breaking swimming records and then will be listed in the International Swimming Hall of Fame in Fort Lauderdale, Florida.

—Sam Freas, President
International Swimming Hall of Fame

◄ Mark Spitz, the great Hall of Famer, is resting on the diving block. He won seven gold medals, the all-time record, in the 1972 Olympics for the United States.

Eleanor Holm won the gold medal for the United States in the 100-meter backstroke event in 1932. She became the nation's most celebrated sports heroine and went on to star in aquatic shows all over the world.

Johnny Weismuller won gold medals for the United States in the 100-meter and 400-meter freestyle events in the 1924 and 1928 Olympics. As a very famous sports hero, he went on to play the role of Tarzan in many popular movies.

ABOUT SWIMMING

Why do swimmers get faster every year? Why do records get broken in the pool at nearly every event? It is because coaching and teaching get better all the time. It is because training drills are more scientific than ever. It is because it is easier to get in condition and stay there. Most of all, it's because swimming can be so much fun.

"I like the fact you can always challenge yourself and always push yourself," says Art Cassidy of the North Rockland Aquatic Club in New York, who has been swimming races for 10 years. "I personally found a lot of enjoyment from setting goals and achieving them.

After a hard workout, it's a great feeling knowing you did something you set out to do, and it's a great feeling not giving up before you get it done."

Americans swim for enjoyment more than they play basketball or bowl or skate. It is the most popular recreational sport in the United States, by far.

"It's not surprising when you think of how many people go to a pool during the summer," says Matt Farrell, Communications Coordinator of U.S. Swimming, which runs amateur swimming in this country. "It is a very popular activity, a pretty good base from which to draw swimmers."

◀ Don Shollander was only 17 when he broke the world record for the 200-meter freestyle. He broke more than 20 world records during his career. Don won four gold medals at the 1964 Olympics and two more in 1968.

There are many groups and federations through which young people get started in swimming. The main organization is:

U.S. Swimming
One Olympic Plaza
Colorado Springs, CO 80909
(719) 578-4578

U.S. Swimming divides the country into four regions: East, West, Central, and South. Each of those areas has local swimming committees (LSC). There are 59 committees covering all 50 states.

The LSCs are in charge of thousands of swim clubs that register with U.S. Swimming. The coaches at these clubs must pass training courses before they can teach the sport. When you contact a swim club, make sure it is registered with U.S. Swimming.

YMCAs, YMHAs, YWCAs, and YWHAs also have official swimming programs. So do many town pools, some schools or religious organizations, Boy Scouts and Girl Scouts, and boys and girls clubs. Here are some addresses and phone numbers that might be helpful for getting more information on the sport:

Young Men's Christian Association
P.O. Box 447
Union City, IN 47390
(317) 964-3185

American Swimming Coaches Association
301 SE 20th St.
Fort Lauderdale, FL 33316
(305) 462-6267

Swimming Canada
1600 James Naismith Drive, Suite 503
Gloucester, Ontario K1B5N4 Canada
(416) 748-5673

"Probably the first thing to do is try to find a local club in your area," Farrell says. "You can call U.S. Swimming, which can help you contact the chairperson of the LSC, and they can say, 'OK, call this number and ask for this person.' They can get you in touch with people in your local area."

Even if you can't or don't want to join a club, you still can be taught race swimming at clinics. U.S. Swimming and the local clubs hold all types of clinics and workshops for parents, officials, coaches, and, of course, swimmers.

"We run what we call a Gold Medal Clinic," Farrell says. "We will take two or three former Olympians or active Olympians and send them to a clinic in different towns. They talk, and they give stroke clinics. This is a great example of people at the top of the sport today teaching the youngsters who someday might be swimming champions competing in the Olympics."

The history of the sport of American swimming is filled with great stories of young swimmers who went on to high achievements. The greatest are ultimately nominated to the International Swimming Hall of Fame. Outstanding superstars Eleanor Holm, Johnny Weismuller, and Mark Spitz are but a few of the names who have brought glory and fame to swimming.

Young students wait for their instructor at a swimming clinic.

ABOUT SAFETY

Unlike sports played on land, swimming has an added dimension of safety. While water sports and games are great fun, they shouldn't be played before everyone is at ease in the water.

There are many tips that help new swimmers learn to be safe swimmers and remind experienced swimmers how important it is to be careful in the water. Because this book deals with race swimming, we will look more closely at safety measures for pools. Here are a few good common sense rules for swimming:

Never swim alone. Always have a strong swimmer around; an adult is best. Use the buddy system, in which two, even three, or more swimmers stay together.

Know the water. Don't swim in strange lakes, ponds, bays, rivers, or at ocean beaches. Make sure someone with you knows the body of water. That person should know how deep it is, how rough the water gets, and they should know if there are rocks or plants, fish or turtles, even eels, crabs, or lobsters. It's important to know if the water is clear or cloudy, if there are waves or currents, and how strong they are. Also find out if there are boats around.

Know yourself. Don't try to swim too far or go into water that is too deep for you. If a lifeguard warns you about something, always listen, even if you believe you are a strong enough swimmer to avoid problems.

Protect yourself from the sun. A tan is nice, but staying in the sun too long leads to trouble. Sun burns the skin and has long lasting effects. Some people figure they can just go into the water to cool off, but that doesn't get you out of the sun.

Don't panic. If there is trouble, think clearly about what to do. Use common sense, the best safety gear of all. Never call for help when you don't need it. If someone else really does need help, you could cause more problems for everyone.

If you get a cramp, and you are far from the shore, it is very important to relax and try to get to a safe place. If the cramp is in your leg, you might be able to rub it out as you head for shore. On shore you can get the right kind of help for different types of cramps.

If the weather turns bad, get out of the water right away. Even an Olympic swimmer does that. It's just the smart thing to do.

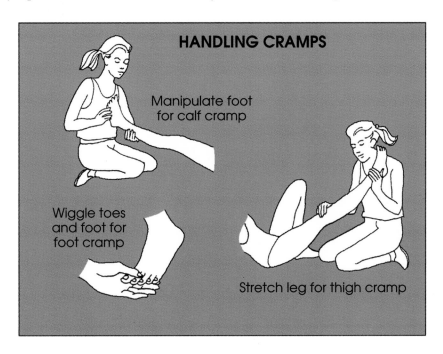

HANDLING CRAMPS

Manipulate foot for calf cramp

Wiggle toes and foot for foot cramp

Stretch leg for thigh cramp

SWIMMING GEAR

Swimsuits: For recreational swimming, there are many styles to choose from at your local department store or sporting goods store. Competitive swimmers wear racing suits, which are lightweight and tight-fitting. They are made of nylon or a combination of nylon and spandex or Lycra.

Boys' trunks should have sturdy tie-strings. Boys may use a nylon athletic supporter.

Girls' and young women's racing swimsuits are usually one-piece "X," "Y," or open-back styles.

Caps: For some girls or young women, snug-fitting latex or Lycra caps may be useful. Caps, however, are not needed for pool swimming. Long hair should be tied at the back.

Shoes and cover-ups: A pair of plastic thongs or rubber slip-ons are helpful for walking around pool areas. A T-shirt, a sweatshirt, or a light nylon windbreaker is useful walking to and from the pool.

Earplugs: Molded earplugs can stop water from getting into your ears. It is important to dry your ears carefully after swimming.

Goggles: If your eyes are sensitive to the chlorine in the water, a pair of inexpensive plastic goggles will offer protection. But goggles are not waterproof. Prescription goggles are available.

Nose clip: A nose clip is very helpful for those who don't like water rushing up their noses.

Towels: Two large terry cloth towels are best: one to dry off when getting out of the pool, another to use after your shower.

Soap and other personal care items: A quality moisturizing soap is good for your skin after swimming. Shampoo and conditioner help keep your hair healthy. A comb, brush, and talcum powder should be part of your gear. However, use small containers.

Swim Bag: A zipper-pouched plastic or nylon bag is just right to store and carry your swim gear in. Keep the load as light as you can.

Pool Safety

As for safety around the pool, most rules involve nothing more than common sense.

- Don't dive into shallow water.

- Don't dive or jump in someone's path.

- Don't run on pool decks, which can be slippery.

- Swim in well-lit areas.

- Don't continue to swim if the water makes your eyes tear or your skin break out in a rash. Chemicals used to keep pools clean can bother people. Let someone know if that happens.

There are also some basic rules of safety for practice or competition:

- Don't do too much.

- Make sure workouts aren't too long or tiring.

- Don't swim when injured.

Finally, it is important to know how to help someone who is having problems in the water. Courses in first aid and rescue are given by YMCAs, schools, and swim clubs everywhere. Sign up for one of these courses for your own safety as well as to help others.

3

THE FREESTYLE OR CRAWL

There are four basic swim strokes: the freestyle (or crawl); the back-stroke; the breaststroke; and the butterfly. Each have specific movements that must be mastered for you to become a good swimmer.

Freestyle really means using any stroke. But the crawl is the most popular and fastest stroke. It's also the easiest, which is why marathon swimmers or people trying to swim the English Channel or cross a river use it.

An experienced swimming coach may tell you to think of a windmill. Think about how a windmill's arms move so smoothly. That is the way to do the freestyle or crawl.

While it looks easy, there are many elements to a proper freestyle stroke. You use your whole body in a freestyle stroke. You stretch your body out as flat as possible in the water. The correct position for the crawl is to float like a log. Your face is in the water, up to the bottom of the forehead. You are looking ahead and just a bit downward.

Now you are ready for your first stroke. Each freestyle stroke has five parts:

1. Entry   **4. Follow-through**
2. Catch and grab   **5. Recovery**
3. Push and pull

If one part of the stroke is done incorrectly, the whole thing will be off. It is important to learn all five parts.

Entry

Your arms will supply most of your movement. During the entry stage, the arm enters the water in front of your shoulder, fingertips first, with the hand facing outward a bit. Your elbow should be bent. The arm moves forward and downward until it is all the way in front of your head. Make sure that the entry is easy and you aren't slapping the water. There should be no splash.

THE CRAWL

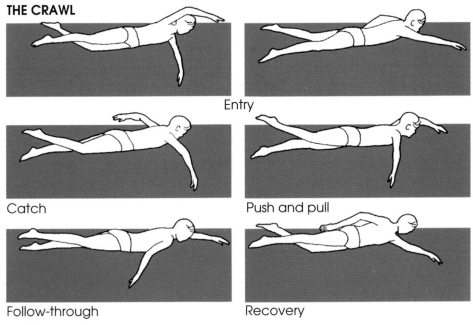

Entry

Catch

Push and pull

Follow-through

Recovery

Catch

Next comes the catch. With your hand facing your feet and the fingers pointing toward the bottom of the pool, turn the wrist so that it seems like all the water in the pool is caught behind your hand. Grab the water with an open hand and your entire arm.

Push and Pull

With the elbow high, the bent arm pulls past the shoulders and under the body. It is pushing the water backward as the arm becomes fully extended in the direction of your feet. As you are doing this, the speed of the hand movement gets faster.

Follow-through

In the follow-through the arm keeps moving past your hips and becomes fully extended. At this point, the other arm has begun its entry.

Recovery

The lead arm is going into the recovery, with the elbow coming out of the water first just as the other arm is doing the catch. The shoulder, then the hand, follows the elbow out, with the hand just above the water. The beginning of the next stroke comes with the end of the recovery, when your hand enters the water again.

A key to the crawl is the body roll. It happens automatically, but you can train the body to help even more by rolling in a relaxed manner. At the time of entry by your right arm, your body should roll toward the right. The hips do most of the work. When the left arm is beginning the stroke, the body rolls to the left. It's important that the roll happens when the arm is entering the water. That makes the stroke stronger, faster, and more fluid.

FREESTYLE EVENTS

Tom Jager is the world-record holder in the 50 meters, the fastest race in the pool. He calls the freestyle events "...the headliners, the races all the fans look forward to. There's so much excitement when the best freestyle racers get up on the blocks and the crowd gets ready for a fast race. It's like when the great runners like Carl Lewis get on the track for their races."

Jager's rivalry with Matt Biondi was one of the highlights of swimming in the last decade. Race after race, they would stroke side-by-side, seeking championships and breaking world records. The waves they churned up looked strong enough to rock a boat.

Jager vs. Biondi became the Muhammad Ali-Joe Frazier matchup of swimming. Two heavyweights in their prime, going head-to-head, producing memorable races and unmatched excitement in the pool.

(Top) Matt Biondi, an exciting racer, won gold medals for the United States in the 50-meter and 100-meter freestyle events in the 1988 Olympics.

(Bottom) Tom Jager, who is swimming in the left lane, is a fierce competitor. He won the world championship in the 50-meter freestyle in1986 and 1991.

Breathing

While your arms are busy and your body is rolling, your head isn't just along for the ride. By turning it to the side, you can get your mouth out of the water. Take a quick breath, and turn the head back to its position. Look ahead and a bit downward. Keep stroking. As your body rolls to the side on which you want to breathe, turn your head, and inhale again. Each time, let the breath out slowly and completely before taking another breath.

You should breathe on whichever side is easiest for you. Breathing to both sides is great. You should breathe as often as is natural for you. Breathe enough times so you are not holding your breath or running out of air because you waited too long.

Try to breathe in rhythm. This means every two, three, or four strokes. Don't breathe after two strokes one time, after four another, then after three.

Kicking

The legs kick in what is called the flutter kick. That means the legs flutter up and down, one at a time. Again, rhythm is important, so try to have a steady kick. The knees bend a little, and the ankles stay loose as one foot kicks down. As it comes up, the knee is straight, and the foot comes out only so the heel is out of the water. Try not to raise the foot too high out of the water. This slows you down and can throw off the whole stroke.

Don't kick down too deep. Some swimmers find a kick that goes more than 12 inches (30 cm) deep is too far.

You can practice the kick even before you know how to do the freestyle stroke. Get a kickboard, hold it out in front of you, and kick your way around the pool. Think only about the kicking until you feel it is correct.

As with breathing, you might wonder how often to kick. Most often, a six-beat kick is used, in which you kick three times for each stroke an arm makes. For shorter races, many swimmers do only two kicks per stroke.

THE BACKSTROKE

The backstroke might be the least comfortable stroke to learn. Yet it is the most comfortable to do. The hardest part about learning the backstroke is that the swimmer does not see where he or she is going. Not only are you learning a new stroke, but you are also thinking about not bumping your head at the end of the pool.

As a swimmer masters the stroke, it becomes natural to do the same number of strokes on each lap. With practice, worries about crashing into the wall will disappear. Besides, there are backstroke flags hanging above the pool, placed a certain distance from the wall to warn you how close you are. Some swimmers prefer the backstroke because their face is out of the water, making it easier to breathe and keep their eyes open.

The first step in learning the backstroke is learning to float on your back. Imagine lying on your bed with no pillow under your head. Your body should be very close to the surface, with the hips only a few inches underwater. Your body must be straight.

Your head should be still and lying back, with the eyes looking at something above the pool. The ears are just below the water, and

Your head should be still and lying back when doing the backstroke.

the chin is just above it. The surface of the water should be even with the middle of your head. Now, you are ready to move.

The backstroke is a windmill motion. Imagine that your body is a clock. Your head is at 12:00, and your toes are at 6:00. Your pinky is the first finger into the water, at 11:00 for the right arm, 1:00 for the left arm. The hand is turned outward as it enters the water, and your arm will sink about 6 inches (15 cm) before it begins to push backward.

As the arm swings around toward the feet, you are pushing the water. As the stroke is completed, the hand is close to the leg and is facing the bottom of the pool.

While this is happening, the other arm is swinging around in the air. It enters the water at either 11:00 (right) or 1:00 (left). The arm that has finished the stroke is ready for the recovery. Lift it straight up. When it reaches its highest point, the hand should be in position for the little finger to enter the water first when the arm comes down.

That arm keeps going. The pinky enters the water as the other arm is down by the leg. This completes one full stroke cycle.

Just as with the freestyle, the body is helping by rolling toward the side of the arm that is pulling. Don't think about the rolling, because the body does it automatically. The legs and feet also help. But because you are on your back, the toes will kick up instead of down. The knee is bent a bit as you do a flutter kick up. As you kick down, your knee should be straight. As with the freestyle, you don't want much splashing.

THE BACKSTROKE

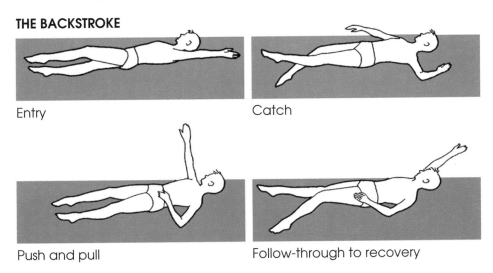

Entry

Catch

Push and pull

Follow-through to recovery

THE BERKOFF BLASTOFF

In 1987, a junior at Harvard named David Berkoff decided there was a better way to do the backstroke. Berkoff won the NCAA college title in the 100-meter backstroke by swimming more than half the pool underwater at the start. That strategy became known as the Berkoff Blastoff and was much faster to use than the normal backstroke.

In 1981, the organizations that make the rules for swimming decided the distance a backstroker could go underwater would be limited to the first 15 meters of each lap. Berkoff did it in the 1988 Olympics but lost the 100-meter race to a Japanese swimmer who used the technique. The Berkoff Blastoff was ineffective after that and disappeared from race swimming.

THE BREASTSTROKE

The breaststroke is different from the other main strokes for a few reasons. When you do the breaststroke, your arms and legs are underwater all the time. It's the only stroke in which this happens. Some people call it the "invisible stroke." From outside the pool, you can't always see the strokes and kicks.

This stroke allows you to see where you are going all the time. The eyes should usually be looking at the hands as they move.

The body is stretched out to begin the breaststroke. The arms reach out to the front as the heels move forward toward your rear end. The legs are only about 6 inches (15 cm) below the water.

The legs are just as important as the arms when you do the breaststroke. Your feet should be as far apart as you can get them. The toes face outward, and the knees are inside the heels. Then both feet kick back at the same time moving quickly. This is called the frog kick.

As the swimmer gets better with the frog kick, he or she might try the whip kick. The feet go out, down, and then in a circling motion in the whip kick.

◀ Lori Heisick is competing in the 200-meter breaststroke event at the Spring Nationals.

You should practice kicking without doing the stroking until you get both legs moving together smoothly. If each leg is working separately, it will slow you down and tire you more quickly. Once you've learned the kick, move on to the arm movements.

With the hands about 6 inches (15 cm) underwater, reach forward. Your hands will be facing out. Sweep your arms out in a circling motion, with the hands moving quickly through the water. Keep your legs stretched out. This arm motion then brings the hands toward your head. They come together under the chin. Then you slide them forward easily as the kick is being done.

THE BREASTSTROKE

Glide

Sweep hands out, lift head

Sweep hands down, legs straight

Sweep hands in, face palms

Turn feet, kick out, sweep out

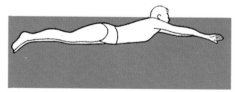

Start the stroke again

Jeff Cummings competed in the U.S. National Championships in the 200-meter breaststroke event.

Now, do the arm and leg movements in rhythm. Remember, when the arms are pulling, the legs are not kicking. When the legs are kicking, the arms are gliding ahead of you to get ready for the next stroke.

Breathe in the middle of every stroke. As the arms are pulling back, take in air. As the hands circle under your chin, put your head into the water, with only the forehead and top of your head above the water. Let the breath out as the arms glide forward to prepare for the next stoke. As your arms pull back, breathe again.

"The breaststroke can look awfully strange," says Steve Lundquist, one of the all-time greatest American breaststrokers. "It's the slowest of the strokes, too. But I always liked it. And it was pretty good to me."

THE BUTTERFLY STROKE

Few movements in a swimming pool have the beauty and grace of the butterfly stroke, especially when it is done the right way. The butterfly is the newest race stroke. It did not become an Olympic event until 1956.

The butterfly stroke is the only one that uses the dolphin kick. This kick is done like the freestyle flutter kick, but both legs do the kicking motion at the same time.

In the starting position, which is like the floating position for the freestyle, your arms reach all the way out front. Your face is in the water up to the eyebrows. Bend both knees a bit. This is called flexing. This will bring your heels up toward the surface of the water. Now drop your hips while straightening your legs and kicking all the way out to the rear. Point your toes as you finish the kick. This kick takes lots of practice to master. It is also the hardest to learn. Try doing it with a kickboard, but don't push down on the board as you kick. Instead, keep your shoulders low and your hips high.

Remember, the dolphin kick is done while you are stroking with your arms, helped by your body. The parts of the stroke are the same as in the freestyle:

1. Entry　　　　　　**4. Follow-through**
2. Catch and grab　　**5. Recovery**
3. Push and pull

(Top) Mary T. Meagher, 100-meter and 200-meter butterfly stroke gold medalist in the 1984 Olympics, is considered one of the greatest American swimmers. (Bottom) Tracy Cawlkins, shown here in the butterfly lap, won two gold medals for the United States in the 1984 Olympics in the 200-meter and 400-meter individual medleys.

First, extend both arms to the front. Your hips should be just a few inches below the water. Lay as flat as you can on the surface of the water. Your arms are going to do the stroke together. Put them into the water just wide of your shoulders and with your elbows a little bit above your hands. This is how you do the downbeat of the first of two dolphin kicks that go with the stroking.

Do the catch with your hands facing down at shoulder width. Slide your hands to the side and down. Right away, bend your wrists and elbows a bit for the grab.

With your elbows still bent, pull your arms back and down to your waist. Push the water back at the same time. Let go of your breath.

When you start the follow-through, your arms come to your side, your head juts out of the water, and you breathe in. While you are taking the breath, your legs are kicking down. Your hands have moved almost straight back past your hips.

For the recovery, relax your wrists, and raise your elbows out of the water. The power from the dolphin kick and your body movement should carry your arms up. Sweep them barely over the surface of the water and toward the front.

THE BUTTERFLY STROKE

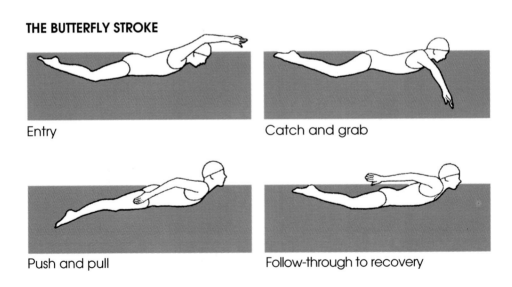

Entry

Catch and grab

Push and pull

Follow-through to recovery

For beginners, a breath might be needed every stroke. When a swimmer has done the stroke for a long time, he or she might breathe every few strokes. Then there is U.S. champion Mel Stewart, who likes to swim most of the 100-meter and 200-meter butterfly underwater, using the dolphin kick. "It's so fast, it's scary," he says. However, unless you are ready for the Olympics, stick with the basics.

Becky Crowe, taking a breath between strokes, won a gold medal in the 1992 United States Olympic Festival swimming the 200-meter butterfly event.

RACE TURNING

No matter how strong you swim, you are not going to win many races if you can't turn. Although it doesn't involve stroking, race turning is very important.

For each of the four strokes, there is a different way to turn. We will look at freestyle, breaststroke, butterfly, and backstroke turns. You can practice turns by themselves. You do need to do some stroking to get into position for them. Spending one portion of a workout just on turns is a good idea.

The Flip Turn

A long time ago, swimmers would touch the wall. They would then make a sideways turn to head back the other way. No one does that anymore, because the flip turn is so much faster.

The flip turn is, simply, an underwater flip that gets you going back where you came from in the quickest time. Done right, it isn't even tiring, and you barely slow down. It is used in the freestyle stroke.

When you get close to the wall, stop the recovery portion of your stroke for one arm. Leave it at your side, with your hand next to your thigh. Make the final stroke with the other arm. Then place it by your side. Both hands should be facing the bottom of the pool.

To flip, duck your head and your shoulders. Push down with your palms. Now do a dolphin kick, as in the butterfly stroke, with your hips dropping while you put your legs straight out. Kick them all the way out to the rear. Finish the somersault by bringing your legs over the top. Move your hands toward your head.

Now you are facing the surface, with your legs by the wall. Plant your feet on the wall. Push off as strongly as you can, getting the power from your legs. Your arms are helping, too, by being stretched past your head.

As you push off the wall, put your body in the right position. Twist so the front of your body is facing the bottom of the pool, and begin kicking as your head breaks out of the water. Begin your normal stroke again.

THE FLIP TURN

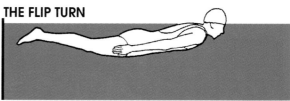

Place stroking arms next to the thighs

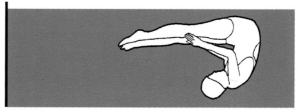

Drive head underwater

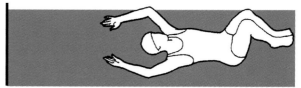

Facing surface, put feet against wall

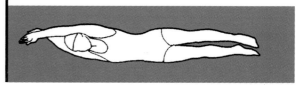

Push off wall

While there are many parts to the turn, the whole thing takes a very short time. Learning how to turn fast will help you win races.

The Breaststroke Turn

The turn for the breaststroke is nothing like the flip, which is not allowed for breaststrokers under current rules. The turn might be more important in the breaststroke than any other stroke. That is because it gives the swimmer a chance to go farther before taking up the stroking again.

THE BREASTSTROKE TURN

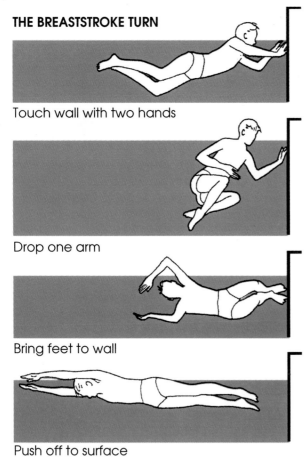

Touch wall with two hands

Drop one arm

Bring feet to wall

Push off to surface

The best time to reach the wall is during the recovery of the stroke. At that time, with the body stretched, you have a full view of the wall. Touch the wall with both hands, not with one, which is against the rules. Use two hands, then drop one arm away from the wall. As you do that, your body will tilt toward that arm, which brings your feet to the wall and your head to the surface. Take a breath, and duck your head back down as you push off the wall hard with your feet.

Stretch out with your arms in front of you. Then take one full stroke underwater, which is allowed by the rules. It is also faster than the normal stroke. Bring your head to the surface as you finish the under-water stroke, then start the whole breaststroke cycle again. During the breaststroke turn, it is important to take a deep breath, because you will be underwater much longer than normal. Actually, practicing this turn can help build your skill at holding your breath.

The Butterfly Turn

Oddly, while the butterfly and breaststroke are not a bit alike, their turns are almost the same. The difference comes only after you have pushed off from the wall. With the butterfly, you go right into the dolphin kick.

Of course, if you are planning on being a world-class swimmer, you might do what Mel Stewart does. He dolphin kicks nearly half the length of the pool before stroking. When he began doing that in 1994, it was legal. But the rules could change any time.

The Backstroke Flip Turn

To do the backstroke flip turn, it would help to know how to do a regular flip. New rules now allow backstrokers to roll over for one stroke just before the turn. That helps you know just where the wall is. But don't touch the wall with your hand. As with the regular flip, the feet will take care of the touch and the push off.

Practice stroking to the wall from the backstroke flags hanging above. That tells you how many strokes you need before starting your turn.

Start with the rollover onto your front. Do it with one crawl, or freestyle, stroke, which is allowed. You should then start the flip. Make sure you are close enough to reach and kick off the wall.

With the flip turn, you wind up on your back. In the freestyle, you must twist your body to get back into position. You are already in position in the backstroke. Put your feet against the wall, and push off strongly, while your arms reach out past your head. Use your flutter kick to get you going. Get your head back to the surface. Then continue backstroking.

BACKSTROKE FLIP TURN

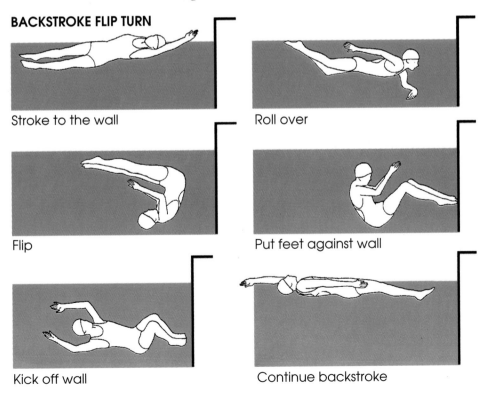

Stroke to the wall

Roll over

Flip

Put feet against wall

Kick off wall

Continue backstroke

Young swimmers practice race diving at a local pool.

RACE DIVING

In a short race, the starting dive can mean the difference between winning and losing. In longer races, the dive doesn't mean as much. Still, it is important to learn the correct way to dive into the pool. You must dive both for safety and to better your chances in races.

Remember that you can practice the dives even without doing any swimming. If you are tired or bored with a stroking workout, stop, and do some race diving. While the dives are alike for the freestyle, breaststroke, and butterfly, some things change with each stroke. The start of the backstroke comes with the swimmer already in the water.

With all dives, the first thing to make sure of is how deep the pool is. It should be at least 7 feet (2 m) deep for safety reasons. Some races might begin without a starting block, but that is rare. Nearly every swim club or swimming event will have starting blocks.

Freestyle Dive

The starter will say "Swimmers up." Get on top of the starting block, and find a comfortable position. Your toes should stick out over the edge of the block. Your feet should be as wide apart as your shoulders.

Next, the starter will say "Take your mark." Lean over, and curl your fingers over the edge of the starting block. Position your hands wherever they feel most comfortable.

Nicole Haislett (front), a great racer, on the diving block. She won a gold medal for the United States in the 200-meter freestyle in the 1992 Olympics.

When the race is about to begin, look straight ahead, not at the starter or the other swimmers. A gun or horn will sound, and your first movement will be to snap your hands forward as you spring off the starting block with your feet. Your hands should go straight out, not around in a windup motion.

As you are diving, your head moves down so that your chin is tucked against your chest as your hands enter the water. The body follows, streamlined, or as flat as possible. Do not make a big splash. The smaller the splash, the smoother you get into the water, and the quicker you can begin stroking.

To get into the stroke, you first must kick strongly as you go forward, which will get you to the surface quickly. Remember, no deep dives, and no belly flops.

Breaststroke Dive

Nearly everything is done the same way as for the freestyle. It is not until you are in the water that the dive changes.

Let yourself dive deeper for the breaststroke, because you are allowed to do a complete cycle of stroking underwater. You can begin the stroke right away instead of moving to the surface to start, as in the freestyle.

With advanced swimmers, the dive and first stroke might cover half the pool before taking a breath. The dive can be a great edge for this stroke.

Butterfly Dive

Again, the same dive is used as in the freestyle and breaststroke. As with the breaststroke, the difference comes in the water.

After entering the pool with a very flat dive, take a few short but hard dolphin kicks. As you take them, get into the starting position for the stroke.

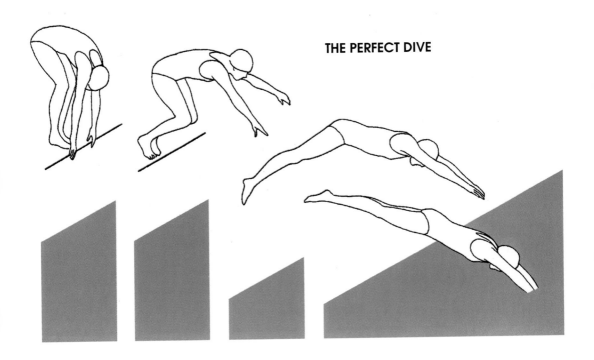

THE PERFECT DIVE

Backstroke Dive

If diving into the pool isn't your thing, maybe the backstroke is for you. Do not think the start is easier just because you begin in the water.

Rules keep changing for the backstroke. The rules today say your feet must be underwater for the start, so keep them as close to the surface as possible.

Put your feet against the wall, and when you hear "Swimmers up," grab the grip bar that is part of the starting block. It should be easy to reach.

When the starter says "Take your mark," pull yourself up almost into a ball. It is a hard position to be in, but it lasts a very short time before the horn or gun sounds.

Royce Sharp is executing a backstroke dive. He was national champion in the 200-meter backstroke event.

At that sound, move your head back, and swing your hands out to the side as you push off the wall with your legs. Your back will bend, or arch, which helps you enter the water as far into the pool as you can stretch.

Again, the entry is not deep and should not be a big splash. The hands, reaching all the way back past the head, enter the water first. The upper body and the legs follow. As you get completely into the water, take a few flutter kicks. This will bring you to the surface and right into your stroking.

A smooth start to a race can be a big advantage for a swimmer. It gives you confidence. It can make your opponents spend extra energy trying to catch up at the beginning of the event. By the end of the race, they might have wasted some energy, and you might be standing on the medals podium because of it.

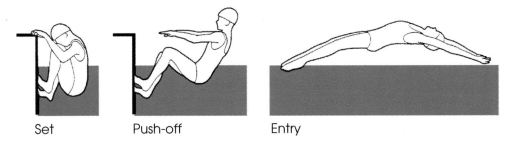

Set   Push-off   Entry

THE BACKSTROKE DIVE

THE MEETS AND BEYOND

All the hard training and long practice hours are aimed at competing in the meet. In a normal season your swimming club, team, or organization will have many scheduled meets. You and your team or club will be competing for prizes, honors, and speed records.

Even the greatest swimmers, from Mark Spitz to Janet Evans, started modestly. They began in local meets, at swim clubs or high school pools, just as you will. First comes that first race dive into a pool, and then those first strokes in competition.

Your coach or coaches will have worked hard to assist you in your training. They will have prepared you well for the meet ahead. You will be advised about what to eat the night and morning before races. The most likely advice will be not to eat anything two or three hours before your meet. Your breakfast should be easily digestible cereal or toast with not too much to drink.

Coming to the meet in the best and most positive frame of mind is most important. You must see yourself winning your race. There are a number of ways to get ready mentally. One of the best ways to be confident is knowing that you have trained for the meet and are

◀ (Top) Students in freestyle school meets compete for prizes.
◀ (Bottom) Lars Jorgenson was the 800-meter freestyle national champion in 1992.

41

BASIC WARMUP EXERCISES

Sit-ups

Push-ups

Squat jumps

Leg stretches

ready for it. Know your strengths and weaknesses. Have a plan of action for finishing in front.

Proper warm-ups are also important. Make sure you spend time in the pool practicing your strokes before a race. Get used to the temperature of the water. Get familiar with the pool and its surroundings.

Do a lot of stretching to loosen up. Many swimmers find squats and knee bends helpful. Others like to bend over and touch their toes several times. Some swimmers simply reach high over their heads to gets their shoulders and arms loose.

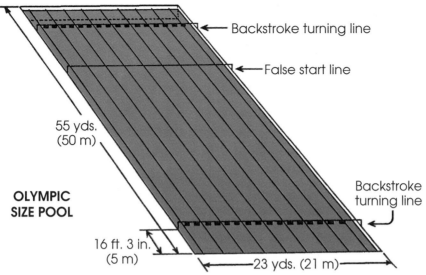

Backstroke turning line

False start line

55 yds.
(50 m)

Backstroke
turning line

**OLYMPIC
SIZE POOL**

16 ft. 3 in.
(5 m)

23 yds. (21 m)

The Rules

An international swimming organization, the Federation Internationale de Natation Amateure (FINA), founded in 1908, establishes the rules for all international events. It oversees the Olympics and world championships.

The pool is divided into eight lanes with numbers going one to eight from left to right. Each swimmer must remain in his or her own lane. In all the events, with the exception of the backstroke, swimmers start the race by diving into the water from starting blocks.

Bathing suits must be in good taste. The referee may disqualify any swimmer whose suit does not meet with the standard.

STANDARD OLYMPIC SWIMMING EVENTS

Freestyle: 50 m, 100 m, 200 m, 400 m, 800 m (women), 1,500 m (men)
Breaststroke, butterfly: 50 m, 100 m, 200 m
Backstroke: 50 m, 100 m, 200 m
Individual medley (equal laps of each of the four strokes):
  200 m, 400 m
Freestyle relay (four swimmers doing equal number of laps):
  4 x 100 m, 4 x 200 m
Medley relay (four swimmers, one doing each of the strokes):
  4 x 100 m

At the Olympic and world championships meets, there are eight officials with the referee being in charge. At school and other club meets there are fewer officials.

At the start of a race, all swimmers step up to the back of the starting blocks, the exception being the backstroke. At the starter's call, the swimmers step up to the front of the blocks and take their positions. The starting signal may be a whistle or the shout "go."

In each of the events the competitor who has qualified with the fastest entry time is appointed the center lane, or, in pools with an even number of lanes, the lane right of the center lane. The swimmer with the second and third fastest entry are placed left and right of the first and so on. The slowest entrants are on the end lanes. This is called the spearhead principle.

Competitors may be disqualified for many reasons. Among them are three false starts, obstructing another swimmer, swimming out of his or her lane, abusive language, and not following directions.

Events in the United States are run by U.S. Swimming. College swim meets are run by the National Collegiate Association of America (NCAA).

The Olympic gold, silver, and bronze medals are the highest honors that championship-level swimmers can strive for. This goal starts early in the minds of most young competitive swimmers. Yet, while very few swimmers will ever compete at this level, it is worth the effort.

A DON SHOLLANDER TIP

"In a sprint, your goal is to maintain maximum speed from start to finish. It's even more important in sprints (short races) than in distance events to warm up before the race. Move your muscles to loosen them; you might possibly even do a little relaxed swimming before the contest begins. Once your race starts, try to get away quickly and powerfully, building to your sprint speed as soon as possible."

Among her many honors and titles, Janet Evans won three Olympic gold medals in 1988 in the 400-meter, 800-meter, and 400-meter individual medley for the United States.

Commitment and Values

Competitive swimming is hard work. Practice and training will take many years. It is not for the weak of mind, spirit, or body. Swimming is a sport you must love. You must enjoy the commitment and dedication required.

Winning races is the goal, but swimming teaches other values. Those long hours of great effort in the water will mold your body. They will refine and focus your thoughts. They will uplift your spirits.

At the end of your competitive career, you will have a healthy body that will be admired. You will possess inner discipline and confidence. You will have formed a respect for all competitors by knowing what is required to enter any race in any sport.

You will know the value of teamwork, the joys of victory, and the disappointment of defeat. The network of friendships you will develop in your chosen sport will always be yours and always be special.

FIND OUT MORE
U.S. Swimming Affiliates

U.S. Swimming has many affilliated organizations that serve the special needs of young people, beginner and advanced, of every area of the public. The following are but a few of the many important members who serve the sport of swimming.

The Amateur Athletic Union (AAU) is devoted to the lifelong pursuit of amateur sports. For swimming, it conducts regional competitions throughout the United States and a national competition in a designated city each year. Your local school, Y, or neighborhood swimming club can qualify you for entry. Write to or phone:

Amateur Athletic Union of the U.S., Inc.
Walt Disney World Resort
Lake Buena Vista, FL 32830
(407) 363-6170

Disabled Sports, U.S.A. serves young people with disabilities. With branches throughout the nation, the organization runs educational and competitive youth programs for ages 10 and up with national events. Its swimming program climaxes with the Paralympic Games, which take place immediately after the international Olympic Games. For more information write to or phone:

Disabled Sports, U.S.A.
4506 9th Avenue
Rock Island, IL 61201
(309) 794-7519

For travel and competitive swimming events abroad, Sport for Understanding sponsors summer international exchange programs for teenagers. Swimmers need not be champions but just lovers of the sport. For information about qualifications write to or phone:

Sport for Understanding
3501 Newark Street, NW
Washington, DC 20016
1-800-TEENAGE

GLOSSARY

Backstroke: Any stroke swum on the back

Belly flop: A poorly formed dive where the diver's body hits down flat on the water

Body roll: In the front crawl and back crawl, a rolling motion used during the stroke to give more power to the underwater part of your arm action

Breaststroke: A stroke swum face down where the arms stroke together, as do the legs, alternating with the arm action

Butterfly: A stroke, much like the breaststroke, where both arms and legs work together. The legs kick together in a front crawl-like action.

Catch: The point at which your hand starts to place pressure on the water during the arm action

Entry: The point at which your hand enters the water for its underwater stroke

Follow-through: One arm, fully extended, moves past hips as the other arm begins entry

Freestyle: An event in race meets where the swimmer can use any stroke

Front crawl: The fastest of all the racing strokes swum on the front side. Each arm works alternately, one taking over from the other. The legs also kick alternately.

Grab: The most basic racing start. The push-off uses the hands as well as the feet, giving a quick dive off the block.

Pull: The motion of the arms during a stroke, ending at shoulder level, with the arms bent at the elbow

Push: The remainder of the arm action, continued after the pull and before recovery

Recovery: Final movement of the arm or leg action in which the arm or leg returns to the point from which it started

Stroke cycle: A complete cycle of the arms and legs, in any stroke, which brings you back ready to start another cycle

Warm-up: Exercises used at the beginning of a practice session to prepare the body and mind for more difficult activity

FURTHER READING

Carson, Charles. *Make the Team: Swimming & Diving*. Little, 1991

Gutman, Bill. *Swimming*. Marshall Cavendish, 1990

Nobel, Jim. *Swimming*. Watts, 1991

Sandelson, Robert. *Swimming & Diving*. MacMillan, 1991

Shawm, Mike and French, Liz. *How to Swim*. Seven Hills, 1993

INDEX

DATE DUE

797.2   Wilner, Barry.
WIL
        Swimming